Why Do We Say That?

101 Idioms, Phrases, Sayings & Facts! A Brief History On Where They Come From!

Scott Matthews

Copyright © 2022 Scott Matthews

All rights reserved. No part of this publication may be reproduced, distributed or transmitted in any form or by any means, including photocopying, recording, or other electronic or mechanical methods, without the prior written permission of the publisher, except in the case of brief quotations embodied in critical reviews and certain other non-commercial uses permitted by copyright law.

Trademarked names appear throughout this book. Rather than use a trademark symbol with every occurrence of a trademarked name, names are used in an editorial fashion, with no intention of infringement of the respective owner's trademark. The information in this book is distributed on an "as is" basis, without warranty. Although every precaution has been taken in the preparation of this work, neither the author nor the publisher shall have any liability to any person or entity with respect to any loss or damage caused or alleged to be caused directly or indirectly by the information contained in this book.

The more that you read, the more things you will know. The more you learn, the more places you'll go.

- Dr. Seuss

Six Benefits of Reading Idioms

1. Knowledge
2. Stress Reduction
3. Mental Stimulation
4. Better Writing Skills
5. Vocabulary Expansion
6. Better Communication Skills

ABOUT THE AUTHOR

Scott Matthews is a geologist, world traveller and author of the "Amazing World Facts" series! He was born in Brooklyn, New York, by immigrant parents from Ukraine but grew up in North Carolina. Scott studied at Duke University where he graduated with a degree in Geology and History.

His studies allowed him to travel the globe where he saw and learned amazing trivial knowledge with his many encounters. With the vast amount of interesting information he accumulated, he created his best selling books "Random, Interesting & Fun Facts You Need To Know."

He hopes this book will provide you with hours of fun, knowledge, entertainment and laughter.

BONUS!

Thanks for supporting me and purchasing this book! I'd like to send you some freebies. They include:

- The digital version of *500 World War I & II Facts*
- The digital version of *101 Idioms and Phrases*
- The audiobook for my best seller *1144 Random Facts*

Go to the last page of the book and scan the QR code. Enter your email and I'll send you all the files. Happy reading!

Why Do We Say That? is a concise and comprehensive collection of idioms created for you to have an easy-to-use, go-to guide on how to apply and understand the most beautiful aspects of the English language - idioms, popular sayings, phrases, and proverbs.

My goal was to collect idioms, their meanings, uses, and origins so you would have them all in one place and at your hand, instead of having to search the Internet.

Some of these phrases have many uses and can be traced back to numerous origins, countries, and cultures. Since I aim to keep the form short, some of these fascinating stories had to be condensed or even overlooked.

I hope you have fun and grow to love the English language and its rich history even more.

P.S. Apologies to my British friends, I'm using American English rules here so if you see grammatical rules that don't make sense, that's why.

Contents

1. All roads lead to Rome 1
2. Mark my words 2
3. Paddle your own canoe 3
4. Make a mountain out of a molehill 4
5. In a pickle 5
6. No dice 6
7. Harp on 7
8. In cold blood 8
9. When pigs fly 9
10. Stir up a hornet's nest 10
11. Joined at the hip 12
12. Knock on wood 13
13. Fat chance 14
14. A smooth sea never made a skilled sailor 15
15. In the loop 16
16. Miss the boat 17
17. Get the wrong end of the stick 18
18. Ahead of the curve 19
19. Back to square one 20
20. Bull in a china shop 21
21. Mind your own beeswax 23
22. No spring chicken 24
23. Across the board 25
24. Stand your ground 26
25. Everything but the kitchen sink 27
26. Drop like flies 28
27. Every cloud has a silver lining 29
28. A stitch in time saves nine 30
29. Kick the can down the road 31
30. Call the shots 32
31. On the cards 34
32. Knock your socks off 35
33. A bed of roses 36
34. In a nutshell 37
35. Walking on eggshells 38
36. Spanner in the works 39
37. Brownie points 40
38. Fair and square 41
39. Laughing stock 42
40. Keep your nose clean 43
41. Elephant in the room 45
42. Green thumb 46
43. Jump on the bandwagon 47
44. An ace up one's sleeve 48

45. Out on the town ... 49
46. Wouldn't be caught dead ... 50
47. Born with a silver spoon in your mouth ... 51
48. Fan the flames ... 52
49. Down to the wire ... 53
50. Bare bones ... 54
51. In the nick of time ... 56
52. At odds ... 57
53. Hissy fit ... 58
54. The devil is beating his wife ... 59
55. Add fuel to the fire ... 60
56. Buckle down ... 61
57. Red tape ... 62
58. On top of the world ... 63
59. Pay the piper ... 64
60. Play cat and mouse ... 65
61. Let the chips fall where they may ... 67
62. Mumbo jumbo ... 68
63. Loose cannon ... 69
64. A slap on the wrist ... 70
65. Low hanging fruit ... 71
66. Head over heels ... 72
67. The eleventh hour ... 73
68. Hot Potato ... 74
69. Old habits die hard ... 75
70. In mint condition ... 76
71. Green with envy ... 78
72. Cut the cord ... 79
73. Keen as mustard ... 80
74. Dead as a doornail ... 81
75. Tall story ... 82
76. Hit or miss ... 83
77. Rain or shine ... 84
78. Fight tooth and nail ... 85
79. Piece of cake ... 86
80. Where the rubber meets the road ... 87
81. Square peg in a round hole ... 89
82. Pep talk ... 90
83. Pie in the sky ... 91
84. Bob's your uncle ... 92
85. All ears ... 93
86. Night owl ... 94
87. Jack of all trades ... 95
88. Chew the fat ... 96
89. On the mend ... 97
90. Jump the gun ... 98

91. Halfway house 100
92. Bull's eye 101
93. On a tear 102
94. Read between the lines 103
95. Leg it 104
96. Mum's the word 105
97. Means to an end 106
98. Devil's advocate 107
99. Once bitten twice shy 108
100. To the nines 109
101. When in rome 110

1. All roads lead to Rome

"All roads lead to Rome" is a proverb that means that whatever methods you choose to do something, you will reach the same outcome in the end. It refers to something that is inevitable. This expression comes from the times of the Roman Empire when their roads were built so that they would diverge from the capitol resembling a wheel with Rome at its center. This analogy was already common in the 12th century. Its first printed use comes from the theologian and poet Alain de Lille that stated, "A thousand roads lead men forever to Rome."

2. Mark my words

"Mark my words" is an expression that is used to tell someone to pay attention to and remember what the speaker is saying. We apply this expression to alert someone that what we are about to say is important. On the other hand, "mark my words" often comes before a negative prediction that we are trying to emphasize. For example, we can say: "Mark my words, this will not end well!" This phrase can be found in the 1535 translation of *The Book of Isaiah*. It was meant to describe something ominous or dark that was going to happen.

3. Paddle Your Own Canoe

When you "paddle your own canoe," that means that you are self-sufficient and independent. There are several origin sources found for this idiom. One source points out that the first mention of this phrase appears in *The Selangor Journal: Jottings Past and Present*, from 1807, which described the lack of cooperation between the coffee planters in Malaysia, stating that instead of working together, each planter "paddles their own canoe." Other sources single out the 1844 book *The Settlers in Canada*, written by Frederick Marryat, as the first known use of this expression.

4. Make a mountain out of a molehill

A person who "makes a mountain out of a molehill" is someone who greatly over-reacts when there is a minor problem or exaggerates when describing a problematic situation, making it look much worse than it is. The mountain represents something large, while a molehill, a tiny lump of dirt made by the digging of a mole, represents something much smaller. We use this idiom to describe or respond to someone falsely presenting their problems as great or unbearable and even to scold them for it. The idiom is found in Nicholas Udall's translation of *The first tome or volume of the Paraphrase of Erasmus upon the New Testamente* (1548).

5. IN A PICKLE

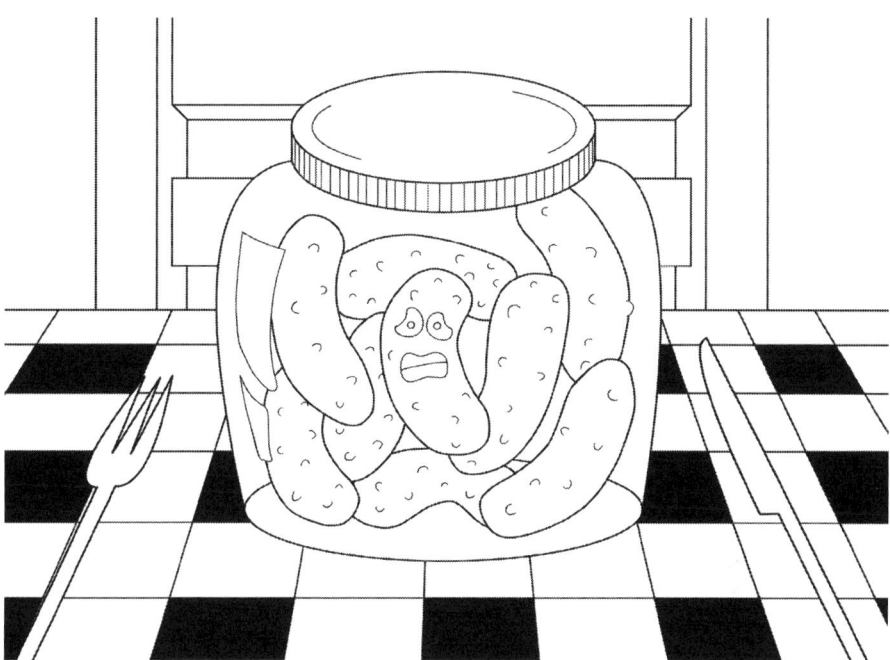

If you're "in a pickle," you're in a difficult position or you have a quandary that isn't easily solved. In the 16th century, the Dutch people had a phrase that translated to "sitting in a pickle" which they used to mean that someone was drunk. Another early usage of "in a pickle" was in Shakespeare's *The Tempest* when the character Alonso asks, "How camest thou in this pickle?" and Trinculo answers, "I have been in such a pickle since I saw you last that, I fear me, will never out of my bones…" which also translated to being drunk. While the origin of the phrase is meant to refer to drunk people, it has since adapted to mean someone is in a tough situation.

6. No dice

This phrase is commonly used to refuse someone's proposal or request, or suggests that there's no chance that something will happen. We can translate this expression as "no chance" and use it if we want to brush off or decline someone's unrealistic suggestion. The phrase first originated in America in the 20th century. Because gambling was illegal in many states at the time, gamblers caught in the act would take their dice and hide or swallow them in order to avoid being charged by the authorities. If the court found "no dice" in their possession, they couldn't make a case against them.

7. Harp on

To "harp on" something means to talk about something continuously or repeatedly in an irritating way. We use this idiom to describe someone's bothersome way of talking, lecturing, complaining, requesting something, or just constantly repeating a topic. The meaning of this expression is connected to the action of continually playing the harp on the same string, meaning "to play the same note over and over." The phrase was used by Shakespeare in several of his plays. In *Richard III*, the character of King Richard uses a variation of the phrase in his line, "Harp not on that string, madam; that is past." In Hamlet, the character of Polonius speaks to the audience saying, "How say you by that? Still harping on my daughter."

8. In cold blood

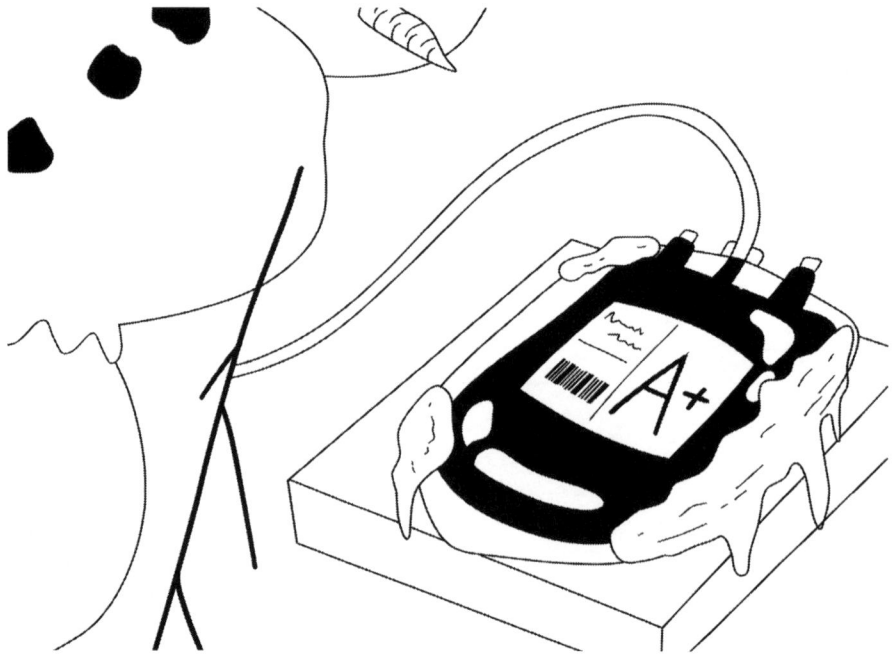

"In cold blood" is an expression that refers to a reprehensible act. For example, when someone is killed for no reason, they are killed "in cold blood." The origin of this phrase can be tied back to 1600s medicine. During that time, it was believed that a person's emotions were connected to the state of their internal fluids. It was a common belief that blood got hotter when someone is angry. Therefore, people with no emotion or regret were thought to have cold blood.

9. WHEN PIGS FLY

The saying "when pigs fly" is a way of expressing one's disbelief that something is possible. We can also use it as a humorous or even taunting response to someone's prediction when we want to let them know that we consider it impossible. For example, in the sentence, "Yeah, your team will win… when pigs fly!" The speaker is saying that the other person's team will never win. This phrase is categorized as an adynaton, a figure of speech in the form of extreme hyperbole in order to imply complete impossibility. Different versions of this adynaton can be found in various cultures such as "when cows fly" in Finnish or "when hens will have teeth" in French. The expression is derived from a centuries-old Scottish proverb, although its most famous use is in Lewis Carroll's *Alice's Adventures in Wonderland*.

10. STIR UP A HORNET'S NEST

To "stir up a hornet's nest" refers to an activity that could result in a negative outcome or provoke someone's negative reaction. We usually apply the phrase "don't stir up a hornet's nest!" when someone is continually behaving in a way that will cause trouble, or to describe someone's actions as risky or instigating. This phrase can be found in *Amphitruo*, a play written by Plautus (200 B.C.), in which the character of Sosia uses it to alert Amphitryon not to get in trouble by arguing with his wife. In English, it can be traced back to the 18th century.

Did you know?

March 1 was designated as the New Year in the early Roman calendar. It had ten months, which is still reflected in some of the names of the months. For example, September through to December, our ninth through to twelfth months, were originally positioned as the seventh through tenth months. *Septum* is Latin for seven, *Octo* is eight, *Novem* is nine, and *Decem* is ten.

Wombats are the only animal whose poop is cube-shaped. This is due to how their intestines form the feces. The animals then stack the cubes to mark their territory.

Eating parts of a pufferfish can kill you because, as a defense mechanism to ward off predators, it contains a deadly chemical called "tetrodotoxin." There's enough in one pufferfish to kill thirty people and there's no antidote. Still, pufferfish, called "fugu," is a highly-prized delicacy in Japan, but can only be prepared by highly-trained chefs.

Early humans used persistence hunting, a technique similarly used by hyenas, wolves and spiders. It involved tracking fast-moving prey over long distances. Humans were partly protected from overheating via exertion because they could sweat, allowing them to endure long runs. That way, they wore down the prey before catching and killing it.

11. Joined at the Hip

To be "joined at the hip" means to be inseparable. We use this idiom as an illustrative and often endearing way of saying that two people are extremely close to each other. One origin idea of this phrase is related to twin brothers Chang and Eng Bunker (1811–1874) who were born with their hips attached. They became recognized for being conjoined twins. The first figurative application of the phrase can be traced back to an article in 1963 from the *Pasadena Star-News* that stated: "The two organizations were so closely knit, they were practically joined at the hip."

12. Knock on Wood

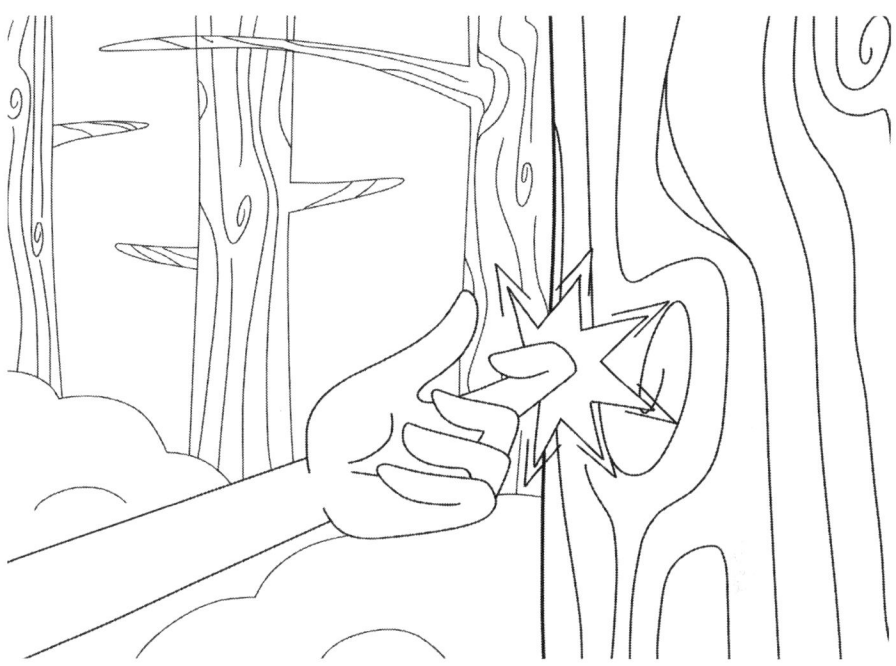

To "knock on wood" is to hope for good luck or good karma. We use this phrase when we want to "invite" good luck to follow us in whatever we're planning to do. People often literally knock on something wooden while saying this expression, as a form of a superstitious ritual that will bring them good fortune. This phrase is thought to come from the ancient Indo-Europeans. People at that time believed the trees housed various spirits, so when you touched the tree, you were given the luck, protection, or blessing of the spirit within the tree.

13. Fat chance

The phrase "fat chance" is a way of sarcastically stating the impossibility of something. When someone tells you that there's a "fat chance" of something happening, they are telling you that there is no chance whatsoever. The origin of this idiom is vague. There are several newspaper articles from the end of the 19th century that used the term "fat chance" which meant "big chance" since the word fat implies that something is ripe and rich. Somewhere along the way, it would seem that the meaning of the expression became the opposite of the word.

14. A SMOOTH SEA NEVER MADE A SKILLED SAILOR

This proverb conveys that life without hardship and the absence of challenges can't help us to develop our character. It's through difficult situations and various temptations that we become more mature and capable. The phrase "smooth sea" represents the easy path through life, while "skilled sailor" represents our virtue and strength of character. This expression is attributed to Franklin D. Roosevelt, the 32nd United States president, but its origin is African.

15. IN THE LOOP

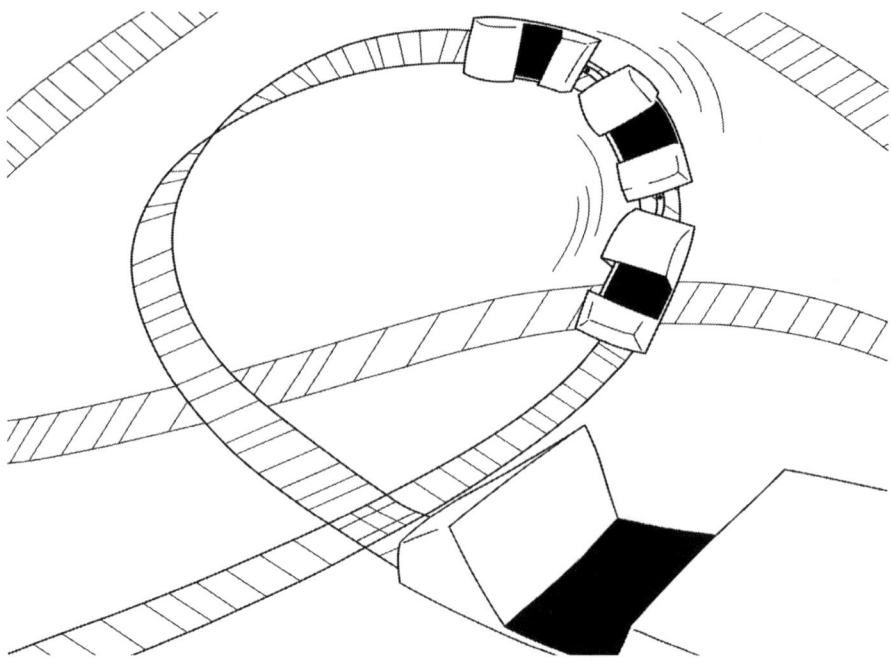

To be "in the loop" means to be aware of particular information. This expression is often formulated as "to stay in the loop," which means to stay informed and acquainted with all the relative aspects within a certain context. In the same way, being "out of the loop" means that a person is not keeping up with the latest information or trends. The origin of this idiom can be traced back to military terminology. In the military, many commanding officers used the phrase "keep everyone in the loop" in the context of passing information to other soldiers to ensure that they were informed.

16. Miss the Boat

When someone has "missed the boat," it means that they have missed their chance to do something by being indecisive or slow to act. However, this idiom can also be used when a person fails to understand something; in this case, we can say that they have "missed the boat" on it. The phrase was first used in a very literal way in Britain when people would miss their boat and be late for their trip. In the 1970s, another popular idiom, "the ship has sailed," was often used interchangeably with this one.

17. Get the wrong end of the stick

A person who has "got the wrong end of the stick" has misunderstood something. We use this expression in a situation when a person has the wrong idea about something that's being explained to them. The imagery of this phrase comes from a walking stick which, when held upside down, doesn't help the one holding it. The original 15th-century version of the phrase was "the worse end of the staff" but it changed to the existing idiom in the late 19th century.

18. Ahead of the curve

A person who is "ahead of the curve" has an advantage compared to others. It can refer to being more prepared, more capable than others, or having an innovative thought before others come up with it. We can also use this expression for a person that has managed to predict something that others could not. This phrase can be found in the *Anchorage Daily News* report from May 22, 1974, during President Nixon's administration, stating that the president and his inner circle used the term.

19. Back to square one

"Back to square one" means returning to the initial starting point. This idiom is commonly used to describe a moment when a process that was advancing in the desired way was stopped, canceled, and brought back to its initial stage, usually by a negative event. The phrase "back to square one" was first used in the 1930s in soccer radio play-by-play. The commentators that were doing the game broadcasts would split the football field into marked grids so that they could explain the plays more easily. The grid that was closest to the home team's goal was marked as "square one." Therefore, if the home team was starting their play from their goal line, the play was called "being back at square one."

20. Bull in a china shop

When a person is like a "bull in a china shop," it means that they are very clumsy. We use this idiom to point out that someone is uncoordinated but in a humorous and kind way. The idea for this phrase comes from the imagery of the bull, a giant animal, in a china shop full of fragile materials made of porcelain. On the other hand, this phrase can also be used to represent someone who is big and brutish. In this case, it doesn't describe a person in a kind way, but rather someone who is too rough. Some sources state that it stems from Frederick Marryat's novel called *Jacob Faithful* published in the year 1834.

Did You Know?

Cartoonist Mort Walker, the creator of Beetle Bailey, came up with images for the things we often see in comics and cartoons. "Briffit" is the dust cloud a character makes when he runs away quickly; "plewds" are the beads of sweat when a character is under duress; and "grawlix" are symbols such as "#@*%" that stand in for curse words.

A mash-up of two words making a new word (such as breakfast and lunch into brunch, or motel from motor and hotel) is called a "portmanteau." In case you're wondering, the word "portmanteau" itself is a portmanteau; it's a compound word that refers to a dual-sided suitcase.

What's inside a Kit Kat? Broken Kit Kats that are damaged during production—they get ground up and go between the wafers, along with cocoa and sugar.

Archaeologists found a ring inside a Viking grave in the 1800s in Sweden that had "For Allah" engraved on it, showing there was linked trade between the Islamic world and the Swedish Vikings from over a thousand years ago.

21. Mind your own beeswax

"Mind your own beeswax" basically means to "mind your own business." In the literal phrase "mind your own business," "business" was converted to "beeswax" to make it less rude and unpleasant. The word "beeswax" has a similar sound as "business" and stands as a proxy for the original word, and even though the message is the same, the form is more socially acceptable. However, there are additional theories about the origin of this expression. The most interesting one tells that beeswax was used as makeup for people who had scars from smallpox during the 18th and 19th centuries and "mind your own beeswax" was a response if someone would rudely stare at their scarred faces.

22. No Spring Chicken

When we say that someone is "no spring chicken," we are saying that that person is no longer young. We usually use this idiom in situations when someone's appearance and behavior create an impression that they are much younger than they really are. In the 17th century, chickens that were born in the spring brought in more money than other chickens because they were younger than those that had lived through the winter. As a result, many farmers tried to sell their old chickens as "spring chickens" which led to people creating the phrase, "that is no spring chicken!"

23. Across the Board

If something is "across the board," that means that it includes or affects everything or everyone within a certain group. For example, having an "across the board" pay raise means that everyone in a certain company will have their paychecks increased. This idiom is commonly used to describe processes that affect all of the people within a party. The expression's origin comes from horse racing as it described a form of betting. An "across the board" bet meant that equal stakes of money were bet on the same horse to either win, place, or show (betting on all categories that were on the board). The idiom was first used in print with this purpose in the *Atlanta Constitution* in November 1901.

24. STAND YOUR GROUND

To "stand one's ground" means to not retreat, falter, or surrender. We can use this idiom in several different contexts. Firstly, "stand your ground" is a common military and war-related phrase, referring to soldiers remaining in their position when the enemy attacking may be stronger or have overwhelming force. In everyday situations, it means someone is ready to defend their intentions, behaviors, or opinions, even when there is opposition by other people. In the world of law, the phrase represents a principle that allows a person to use deadly force in self-defense without first trying to retreat. The first "Stand Your Ground" law in America came to pass in Florida in 2005 and they now exists in over thirty states.

25. Everything but the kitchen sink

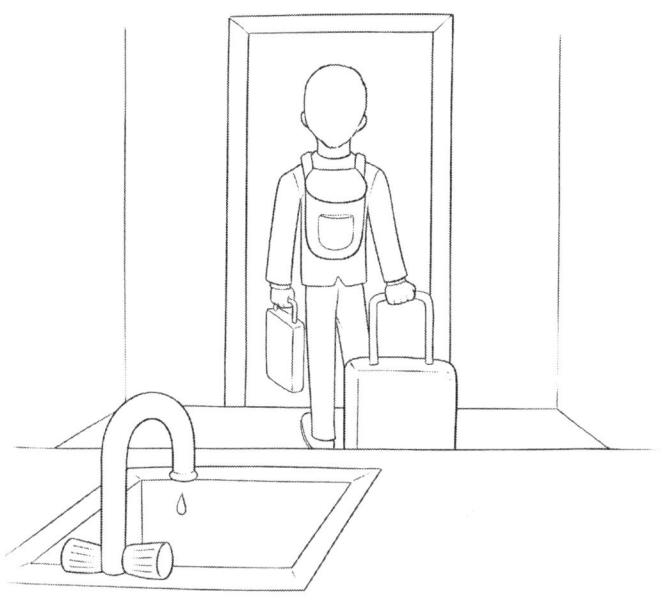

This is a phrase that is jokingly used when someone has overpacked for a trip. In this situation, we can say that they have packed "everything but the kitchen sink." It translates as "everything imaginable" or "much more than necessary." The first use of this idiom can be traced back to the early 20th century in the newspaper *The Syracuse Herald*. The phrase "everything was thrown at the enemy, but the kitchen sink," was popularly used during World War II in descriptions of battles. However, there's an even older expression, "everything but the kitchen stove," which dates from the 19th century and could be this one's predecessor.

26. Drop like flies

The expression "drop like flies" means that people or animals are falling dead or ill very quickly in large numbers. While the origin of this idiom isn't entirely certain, it is clear that this phrase represents the short lifespan of a fly. Namely, flies have a maximum lifespan of twenty-eight days, so they die and drop very quickly and easily. One of the recorded uses of this phrase was the 1902 *Atlanta Constitution* newspaper reports on a fire that broke out that, "I saw men and women rushing back and forth within the flames. They would run along, then came the choking smoke and they would drop like dead flies."

27. Every cloud has a silver lining

This proverb states that we can find something hopeful and comforting in every challenging or sad situation, even if we can't see it at the moment. We usually use this proverbial saying for the purpose of comforting someone who is going through hardship or to inspire them to "look at the bright side." This idiom has most likely been traced back to 1634 when John Milton stated, "Was I deceived or did a sable cloud turn forth her silver lining on the night?"

28. A Stitch in Time Saves Nine

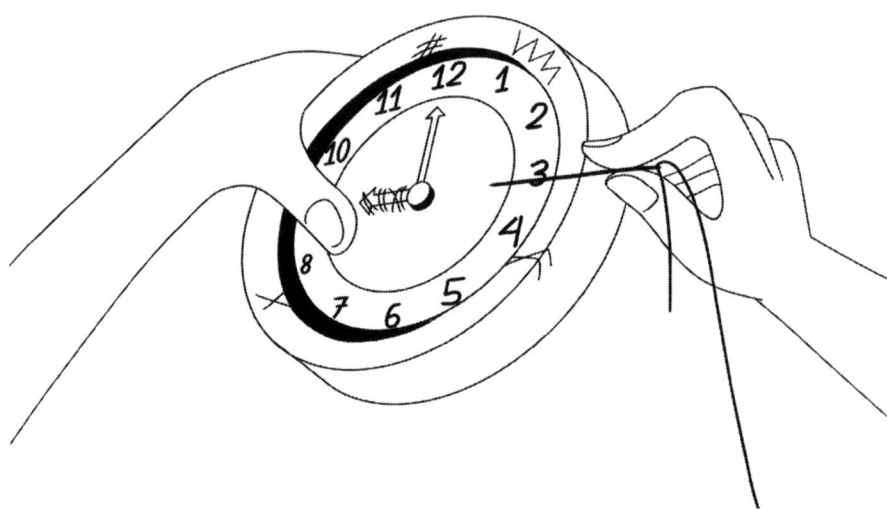

This proverb states that it is better to resolve a problematic situation when it is still a little nuisance than to wait until it becomes a serious crisis. We usually use this proverbial expression when we want to urge someone to take care of a problem immediately before it grows or to simply point out that such an approach to life can save us a lot of time and trouble in the future. This phrase was first seen in *Thomas Fuller's Gnomologia: A Collection of the Proverbs, Maxims, and Adages That Inspired Benjamin Franklin and Poor Richard's Almanack* in 1732.

29. Kick the can down the road

To "kick the can down the road" means to put off facing a difficult situation or making an important decision. We use this idiom to describe a situation when a person is procrastinating on something vital. Often, it's used when a person has been delaying for a considerable time or when dawdling is typical for that person. The expression originates from a game that was played during the Great Depression. This game was a version of 'hide n seek,' with the rule that kicking the can will release all the players that have been captured during that round. It isn't clear how that translated to its modern meaning. It's more plausible to connect the meaning to the imagery of kicking trash on the street out of sight so it becomes someone else's concern.

30. CALL THE SHOTS

A person who is "calling the shots" is a person in a position of leadership who makes important decisions that will affect a certain situation. We use this idiom to describe an action of making important decisions or to single out a person who is in charge. This expression was part of the military vocabulary. Namely, during marksmanship training, it was common practice to declare where a fired shot had hit the target. Also, some shooters called where they were intending to shoot beforehand. The phrase with its modern meaning was first used in print in the 1960s.

Did you know?

There was a medieval belief that crocodiles shed tears of sadness while they killed and consumed their prey. From this myth, which dates back as far as the 14th century, the term "crocodile tears" is actually derived. The belief started from a book called "The Travels of Sir John Mandeville" and, later on, it was found in the works of Shakespeare.

The teddy bear is named after President Theodore Roosevelt. After he refused to shoot a captured black bear on a hunt, a stuffed-animal maker decided to create a bear and name it after the president.

Play-Doh started out as a wallpaper cleaner before the head of the struggling company realized the non-toxic material made a good modeling clay for children and rebranded it.

The sister ship of the Titanic, the Olympic, offered to take in the survivors when the Titanic sank. The Captain of the Titanic rejected the offer as he was afraid that this would cause panic among the survivors seeing a virtual mirror image of the ship that had just sank, asking them to come on board.

31. ON THE CARDS

If something is "on the cards," it means that it is meant to happen or most likely going to happen. In America, the same idiom is referred to as "in the cards" while in Britain, the phrase is referred to as "on the cards." The origin of this idiom can be drawn back to the 1800s when tarot cards and fortune-telling were rising in popularity. When something was written on the cards in tarot or fortune, it was meant to tell your future. It can also be seen in a poem written by Charles Churchill titled *Independence*.

32. KNOCK YOUR SOCKS OFF

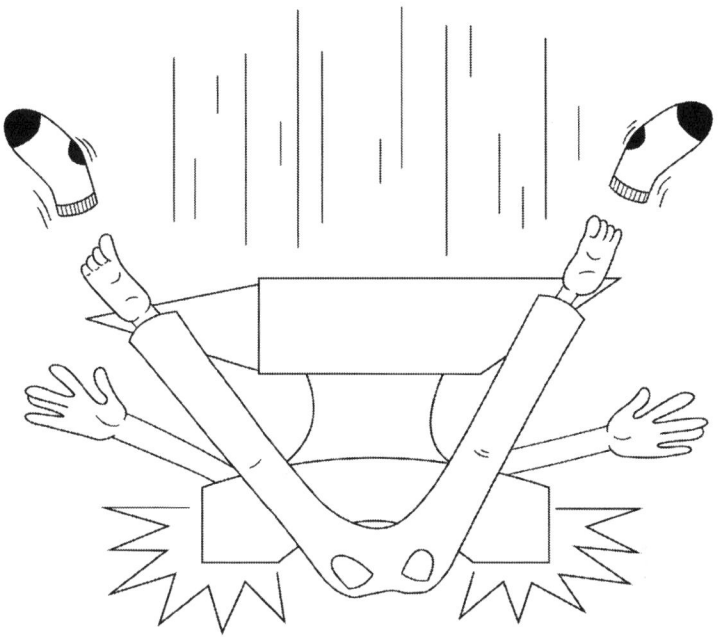

If something "knocked your socks off," it means that you were impressed by it. We use this idiom to describe something exciting or when we want to share our enthusiasm with others, to let them know that they are about to see something amazing. This idiom was originally used in the southern regions of America in the 1940s. During that time, the phrase meant to beat someone in a fight, but it changed from winning a fight to impressing someone.

33. A BED OF ROSES

A person laying in a "bed of roses" is in a very comfortable or luxurious position. We use this idiom to describe someone's favorable circumstances. One of the earliest written forms of this expression can be found in a poem titled *The Passionate Shepherd to His Love* which was published in 1599. The poem stated:

> And I will make thee beds of roses
> And a thousand fragrant posies,
> A cap of flowers, and a kirtle
> Embroidered all with leaves of myrtle.

34. IN A NUTSHELL

The phrase "in a nutshell" refers to telling a story concisely or quickly. We use this idiom when we want to let someone know that what we are about to tell them is a shortened and simplified version of the entire account. This idiom's first use can be found in a book titled *Natural History* by the Roman writer Pliny the Elder. In the book, Pliny describes Homer's *Iliad* as being copied in so tiny a hand that it could fit "in a nutshell." However, it was later found that Shakespeare had used this phrase in Hamlet with the meaning of "something compact," while William Thackeray (British novelist) used it in its present meaning in *The Second Funeral of Napoleon* in 1841.

35. Walking on Eggshells

When a person is "walking on eggshells," it means that they have to be careful with what they are doing or saying. We use this idiom to describe a situation when a touchy subject is being discussed and people have to watch what they are saying and how they are behaving so as to not offend anyone. This phrase came into use in the 1800s after its predecessor "walking on eggs." The phrase stems from the imagery of walking on something as fragile as eggs, which emphasizes how careful that person has to be.

36. Spanner in the Works

To throw a "spanner in the works" is to, purposefully or not, sabotage something, cause its delay or interruption, or to interfere with a certain process or procedure. The phrase can be found in several forms - "put/throw a spanner/wrench in the works/wheels/gears." Its first recorded print is found in *The Parliamentary Debates* of the New Zealand Parliament, 1932: "Of course, every honorable member has a right to express his opinions, even of a critical nature, but I do think we should expect them to help and not throw a spanner in the gears."

37. Brownie points

When a person is trying to make a good impression on someone or establish a positive relationship, they try to earn their respect and trust by doing something nice for them. The term "brownie points" is a representation of all of our nice gestures for someone, which make them think positively of us. This idiom originated from the points earned for different accomplishments by the Brownies, which were the youngest girls within the Girl Scouts. In the mid-20th century, it became an expression used for achievements within any relationship with a person or a group.

38. Fair and square

"Fair and square" means that something is done according to the rules or the agreement between two parties. We use this expression to describe a situation in which every agreed-upon rule has been honored and to state that the outcome is acceptable because it is fair. This rhyming phrase can be traced back to the 1600s and it was used in reference to sports or contests (it is still often used in the same context). The initial phrase was "fair and honest," but over time, the word "square" slowly replaced "honest."

39. Laughing stock

The "laughing stock" of a certain group is the person who is being laughed at by everyone else in the group. We use this expression to state that a person is being ridiculed, made fun of, and even humiliated by others. Calling someone the "laughing stock" of the group can be insulting. The origin of this expression could be related to the stocks: a punishment method that included the guilty person having their head and hands trapped inside a wooden stock. Other people would then ridicule them and throw objects at them for their crimes.

40. Keep your nose clean

The phrase "keep one's nose clean" refers to that person's tendency to stay out of trouble and maintain their good reputation. We use this expression to state that our priority is to have a clean reputation and keep our conscience clean. This phrase was originally worded as "keeping your hands clean." When it was used in England in the 18th century, it related to avoiding corruption. When it was adopted in the United States as "keep your nose clean," it meant to keep your nose out of other people's business.

Did you know?

Michelin stars are highly coveted by elite and upscale restaurants all around the world. They are actually given out by the Michelin tire company, the same one whose mascot is the marshmallow-like Michelin Man.

The longest place name in the world, at eighty five letters, is "Taumatawhakatangihangakoauauotamateaturipukakapikimaungahoronukupokaiwhenuakitanatahu," in New Zealand. Locals just call it Taumata Hill.

The world record for the holder of the most world records is Ashrita Furman, who's set more than six hundred records and currently holds more than 200. His records have ranged from fastest mile on a pogo stick, longest time to hula hoop underwater, and greatest distance traveled on a bicycle balancing a milk bottle on the head.

The first housewarming parties were literally held to warm houses and send the spirits away. All guests would bring over pieces of wood and they would light fires in every fireplace in the new home. There was a belief that empty houses would attract spirits and ghosts, so when people would move in, they would warm the house to send the spirits away.

41. Elephant in the room

When there is an "elephant in the room," it means that there is an obvious issue that no one wants or dares to address. We use this widely known idiom in situations when everyone in a certain group is avoiding a subject, usually because it is touchy and delicate, which causes everyone to feel awkward and unpleasant. Addressing the "elephant in the room," which is also how the phrase is commonly applied, is stating that the subject has to be discussed because it is apparent to everyone and there is no point in pretending. The origin of it stems from the imagery of a huge animal such as an elephant in a narrow space, which would make it impossible to be unnoticed.

42. Green thumb

To have a "green thumb" means that you are good with plants and wildlife. This is an expression that describes people who have an affinity towards gardening, growing plants, and who enjoy spending their time in green environments. This phrase comes from the fact that people who regularly handle plants get their thumbs stained green from algae growing on the exterior of pottery. Because of this, if someone has a "green thumb," others would know that they are often involved with plants.

43. Jump on the Bandwagon

When someone starts liking a celebrity who is at the peak of their fame or starts cheering on a team that is currently winning, they are "jumping on the bandwagon." This expression describes some people's tendency to like, support, and cheer individuals or groups that are currently the most popular, just because the majority of people feel the same. This phrase was first heard in the 1848 presidential campaign of Zachary Taylor. Dan Rice was a popular circus clown at the time who invited Taylor to his circus bandwagon. As he grew in popularity, people began to tell his opponents that they should "jump on the bandwagon" as well.

44. An ace up one's sleeve

If someone has an "ace up their sleeve," that means that they hold a secret advantage in reserve that they can use at any time and without others anticipating it. An ace up one's sleeve can be an object, a skill, or a piece of information that they secretly have, that could better their position in various contexts. The term "to have an ace up one's sleeve" originates from mid-1800s gambling games. Specifically, in a game of poker, the ace card is the most powerful card you can be dealt. Therefore, someone holding an ace up their sleeve would have a secret advantage that they could use to win the game.

45. Out on the Town

Going "out on the town" means that a person is going out to bars and clubs, probably visiting several places for a night out. Usually, people say they are going "out on the town" when they are going out to a party or to have fun. This phrase is thought to have originated in the 1700s, but it didn't gain popularity until the 1900s when a stage show titled "On The Town" was performed in 1944 and a film by the same name, starring Gene Kelly, Frank Sinatra, and Ann Miller, came out in 1949. Since then, it became a common way of expressing our plans of going out and our enthusiasm about it.

46. Wouldn't be caught dead

If a person says that they "wouldn't be caught dead" doing something, it means that they find that action reprehensible or shameful. For example, people often say that they "wouldn't be caught dead" wearing a piece of clothing because they dislike it so much that they would feel embarrassed if they were wearing it. The phrase is meant to convey such an extreme embarrassment of something, that we wouldn't want to be associated with it, even if we were dead. This phrase first appeared near the beginning of the 20th century.

47. Born with a silver spoon in your mouth

If a person was "born with a silver spoon in their mouth," it means that they were born into a wealthy household and have grown up leading a privileged and comfortable life. We usually use this idiom to point out someone's high social and material status, but with certain disapproval, because their wealth and comfort have made them spoiled or lazy. The phrase contains a reference to a spoon because old spoons were made of wood, so only those who were wealthy owned silver spoons. The expression first occurred in print in English in 1719, in Peter Anthony Motteux's translation of the novel *Don Quixote*.

48. Fan the flames

To "fan the flames" means to amplify already strong feelings or to intensify an already tense situation. These feelings can be positive (like love/infatuation), or negative (like anger/resentment). In both cases, if a person does something to stir up those feelings, we can say that they have "fanned the flames." The first use of this idiom in writing was by Charles Dickens in *The Old Curiosity Shop* when he said, "Fan the sinking flames of hilarity with the wing of friendship."

49. Down to the Wire

"Down to the wire" is an expression used to describe a suspenseful situation that's not going to be resolved or decided until the last moment. This idiom is most commonly applied in sports and competitions, where games are often close and the result can be decided at the last second. This phrase is believed to have come from horse racing where there was a wire hung across the finish line. The winner was decided by the horse that touched the wire first, so when the race was close, the result was going to be "down to the wire."

50. Bare bones

When something is "bare bones," it means that it includes only its basic or bare elements. We use this idiom to describe something that includes only what's necessary; for example, the "bare bones" of a novel's plot represent only the key points of its story. This expression stems from the 1700s and, originally, it was related to the description of someone extremely skinny which made it possible to notice the outline of their bones through their skin. Over time, that meaning transformed to breaking something down to its more essential elements.

Did you know?

Competitive art used to be an Olympic sport. Between 1912 and 1948, the international sporting events awarded medals for music, painting, sculpture, and architecture.

English as a second language is four times more common than as a native one. While more people speak English as a second language, nearly three times more people speak Mandarin Chinese natively. Nearly two billion people are learning English as a second language while only 350 million people natively speak it.

When Genghis Khan died, his successors killed anyone who witnessed his funeral procession in order to keep his burial place a secret. About 800 soldiers were massacred as well as 2,000 other people. The location of his tomb is unknown to this day.

The lyrebird can mimic almost any sound it hears. Wildlife watchers have recorded the Australian species copying not only other birds but artificial sounds such as car alarms, camera shutters, and even chainsaws.

51. In the nick of time

"In the nick of time" means just in time. We use this idiom when something has happened in the last possible moment before it was too late, usually when someone arrives or when something is done just before the deadline. This expression originates from the 16th century. However, its predecessor was the phrase "pudding time" because pudding was the dish served first in medieval Britain. To arrive at "pudding time" meant to get there at the start of the feast, just in time to dine.

52. At odds

When two parties are "at odds" about something, that means that they are in conflict or disagreement. We use this idiom to point out that two people or two groups have different stances on an issue or when someone is not approving of a certain action, process, or objective. It's appropriate to say that people are at odds either about/over something, or at odds with each other (if the disagreement lies between people). The origin of this idiom is believed to come from the concept of odd or even. When things were even, they were the same. When things were odd, they were the opposite.

53. Hissy fit

When someone throws a "hissy fit," they are throwing a tantrum as a child would. The expression can be synonymous with an angry outburst. This idiom originated in the 1900s, though it first began as just "hissy." It is believed that the word came as a shorter version of the word "hysterical." Other origin theories make a connection between the phrase and hissing noises related to being angry or aggressive.

54. THE DEVIL IS BEATING HIS WIFE

"The devil is beating his wife" is an idiom that describes a weather occurrence commonly known as a sun shower, when it's raining and the sun is shining at the same time. This expression can be linked to folkloric tales of various cultures. Most of these tales include animals or tricksters being related or getting married to the devil. For example, when a sun shower happens, Hungarians say "the devil is beating his wife with a walking stick," while the French expression is "the devil is beating his wife and marrying his daughter." The imagery of the phrase can be related to the symbols of the devil spitting fire, represented by the sun shining, and his crying wife represented by the rain.

55. Add fuel to the fire

To "add fuel to the fire" means to further instigate an already tense situation that's usually filled with negative emotion, like anger and frustration. We use this phrase when someone's actions don't de-escalate a crisis but make it even more complicated instead. We call those actions "adding fuel to the fire." This expression is of Latin origin and can be traced back to around the year 1 A.D. The Roman historian Livy used this expression in his *History of Rome*.

56. Buckle down

To "buckle down" means to focus and take your work or situation seriously. For example, if a person has a short deadline on an important project at work, they will "buckle down," concentrate, and promptly get their work done. While this modern phrase comes from the United States, there was an older phrase that was similar in Britain that was said as "buckle to." This phrase dates back to the 18th century in a story by John Arbuthnot where it read, "Squire South buckles to, to assist his friend Nic." In America, the first time the modern phrase was in the *Atlantic Monthly* with a quote: "If he would only buckle down to serious study."

57. RED TAPE

Running into "red tape" means that a person is being stopped or slowed in doing something, by rules or regulations. It is most commonly used to refer to unnecessary paperwork in certain processes, particularly in legal or bureaucratic work. It is commonly believed that the phrase came from King Charles V, King of Spain and Holy Roman Emperor, in the early 16th century. During his time, red tape was used to single out the most important documents that required immediate attention by the Council of State and separate them from the other less important issues. That way, the red tape became a symbol of speeding up administrative processes.

58. On top of the world

Being "on top of the world" means that a person feels good, confident, and happy with themselves and how their life is going. We use this phrase to describe a feeling of pleasure with oneself, usually because the person has achieved something that they have dreamed of. This phrase has been around since the 1920s as many writers would use it in their work. It was most commonly phrased as "sitting on top of the world," but it was eventually shortened to just "on top of the world."

59. Pay the Piper

To "pay the piper" means to pay the consequences for one's actions, usually self-indulgent or irresponsible behavior. We use this idiom to describe a situation when someone is feeling the negative effects of their mistakes or to warn someone that their current behavior can lead to bad outcomes and that they will have to "pay the piper" sooner or later. This expression can be traced back to the 1680s from the story *The Pied Piper of Hamelin*. In the story, a man with a pipe appears in town and states that he can solve the townspeople's problem for a price. Once they paid, he led all of the rats out of town.

60. Play cat and mouse

When two parties "play cat and mouse," it means that one or both parties are saying or doing confusing and contradictory things, changing their opinions and behavior towards the other side, or acting deceitfully. The phrase is commonly applied to people and how they treat each other. Namely, when people often change their attitude towards each other, frequently arguing and making up - we say that they are playing cat and mouse. This idiom can also be applied to other kinds of contradictory, avoidant, or deceitful behaviors. The phrase originates from the imagery of a cat's hunt for the mouse. Cats will often play with their prey until it's tired or torment it until it dies. It has been applied in writing since 1675 and can be found in the Brothers Grimm *Fairy Tales*.

Did you know?

The Great Fire of London left more than 70,000 people homeless after destroying more than 13,300 buildings in 1666. Despite all the destruction, only six deaths were verified in official records.

As far back as 200 B.C., the Han Dynasty of China drilled for natural gas, transported it in pipelines and gas containers, and burned it on stoves, though natural gas wasn't in common use worldwide until the 1800s.

Moonflowers actually bloom in response to the moon. Sunflowers will follow the sun as it moves across the sky, but their lunar counterparts only open after nightfall or on cloudy days.

The first Roman fire brigade consisted of 500 men and it was created by Marcus Licinius Crassus. The brigade would show up at a burning building and start haggling with the property owner over the price of their services. If Crassus didn't get a high enough payment offer, he would literally let the building burn to the ground, then he would ask the owner to let him buy it for a fraction of its original value.

61. Let the chips fall where they may

To "let the chips fall where they may" means to let something happen regardless of the consequences. This phrase originated in America in the 1800s. It was first used in reference to chopping wood. Namely, woodcutters used the expression to let each other know that they should proceed with their work without worrying where the chips of wood would end up.

62. Mumbo jumbo

"That's a load of mumbo jumbo!" - this phrase means that something is meaningless or incomprehensible to the observer. It was most commonly associated with religious customs and rituals that people of different religions didn't understand. Sadly, this phrase came to be out of human ignorance. The idiom originates from the Mandingo word "Maamajomboo," which refers to a masked male dancer who was part of African religious rituals. However, people of other religions looked at this character and didn't understand his meaning, thus changing the original name Maamajomboo to the modern "mumbo jumbo."

63. Loose cannon

When someone is a "loose cannon," it means that they are unpredictable and that others don't know what they're going to do next. The expression usually has a negative connotation attached to it because people with such an impulsive character may cause harm to those around them due to their unpredictability. The phrase stems from naval terminology. Back in the 17th century, warships would carry cannons as their primary weapon. These cannons had to be secured with rollers and ropes, and those that became loose and rolled around the deck would present a danger for the crew of the ship if they fired and hurt someone or damaged the vessel.

64. A SLAP ON THE WRIST

Getting "a slap on the wrist" means getting a mild punishment, usually for a larger action or crime, that probably deserved a more severe penalty. The origin of this expression is most likely 18th century England, where the term "slap" was used both literally and figuratively. In 18th century England, punishments for crimes would often be quite severe and of a physical nature. Therefore, a slap on the wrist would have been seen as a light punishment.

65. Low hanging fruit

"Low hanging fruit" is a term that is most commonly used in workplaces or in business for tasks and procedures that can be easily accomplished. We use this idiom to describe work that takes little to no effort. The phrase comes from farmwork and harvesting because the fruit that didn't require harvesters to climb on ladders was the easiest to be picked up. That idea was then translated into any effortless work.

66. Head over heels

To fall "head over heels" in literal meaning refers to turning over completely while going forward, like doing a somersault. However, the more common practise is its metaphorical use, which refers to falling completely in love with someone. To be "head over heels" for a person means to be deeply in love with them. This phrase can be traced back to the 1300s and its predecessor "heels over head" which meant hanging upside down. The phrase was transformed to "head over heels" in the 1700s and started to relate to its present meaning in the 1800s.

67. THE ELEVENTH HOUR

Doing something at "the eleventh hour" means doing it at the last minute. We use this phrase whenever something has been done just before the deadline, like the sentence, "I got there at the eleventh hour," meaning that the speaker was almost late, but made the appointment. The phrase "eleventh hour" has a Biblical background. It comes from a chapter in the *Gospel of Matthew* in which some last-minute workers, who were employed long after the rest, are paid the same salary. Even though they were employed after eleven hours of work, they weren't too late to receive their pay.

68. Hot Potato

"Hot potato" refers to a controversial issue or situation which is awkward to deal with. We use this idiom for a topic that is touchy to discuss or a situation that doesn't have an easy resolution. This expression originates from the imagery of holding or handling a hot potato. One would have to get rid of the potato quickly so they wouldn't get burned, or avoid such a situation completely. Handling a difficult situation or a controversial subject can feel like juggling a hot potato. This term can be traced back to the mid-1800s.

69. Old habits die hard

This proverb states that habits that a person has are not easy to get rid of. It can also mean that someone's behavior is not easily changeable. The most common examples for this expression are found in situations when people are trying to quit smoking, change their diet, or modify some other deeply rooted behavior. We usually use it when these negative behavioral patterns have been present for such a long time, that breaking them represents a great challenge. In some cases, the speaker is trying to express their disbelief that the person in question is capable of change. This proverbial phrase can be traced back to an article written by Benjamin Franklin in 1758.

70. In Mint Condition

Something that is "in mint condition" is completely preserved in its original state. This expression is most applicable to collectors of objects who are very particular about the condition of their collectibles. A collectible object in mint condition has a higher value in the world of collecting. The origin of the phrase stems from the meaning of the word "mint." To "mint" something is to form a shape from a piece of metal. Therefore, to be "in mint condition" is to look fresh and crisp as a newly minted coin. This phrase can be traced back to an 1895 Scottish newspaper that stated that a postage stamp that was in mint condition was being sold for a higher price.

Did you know?

In the Satere-Mawe Indian culture, there is an initiation ritual for thirteen-year-old boys that consists of making them wear gloves made of bullet ants for ten minutes. Although they are repeatedly bitten, which is incredibly painful, they must not cry out if they want to be declared a man.

The Great Sphinx of Giza was constructed out of a single chunk of soft limestone bedrock. This magnificent monument stands over sixty five feet (twenty meters) high, almost two hundred and forty feet (seventy-four meters) long, and over sixty-two feet (nineteen meters) wide.

A team of six women programmed the first digital computer. While historians have only recently recognized their achievements (or many female discoveries credited to men), the female mathematicians participated in a World War II program, coding instructions into the revolutionary Electronic Numerical Integrator and Computer (ENIAC).

Cobwebs actually have antifungal and antiseptic properties that keep bacteria away and minimize the chance of infection. In fact, the Greeks and Romans would use cobwebs to treat cuts in ancient times. Soldiers also used them to heal wounds, combining honey and vinegar to clean the lesions, and then covering them with balled-up spider webs.

71. Green with envy

To be "green with envy" means to be very jealous of someone. The expression is used to emphasize the potency of the person's envy and negative emotion. In ancient Greece, the color green was related to sickness, fear, and jealousy. Because of this, the color green became a common symbol of a person being envious. The phrase was further popularized by William Shakespeare in his famous play *Othello* when he wrote, "Beware, my lord, of jealousy; it is the green-eyed monster which doth mock the meat it feeds on."

72. CUT THE CORD

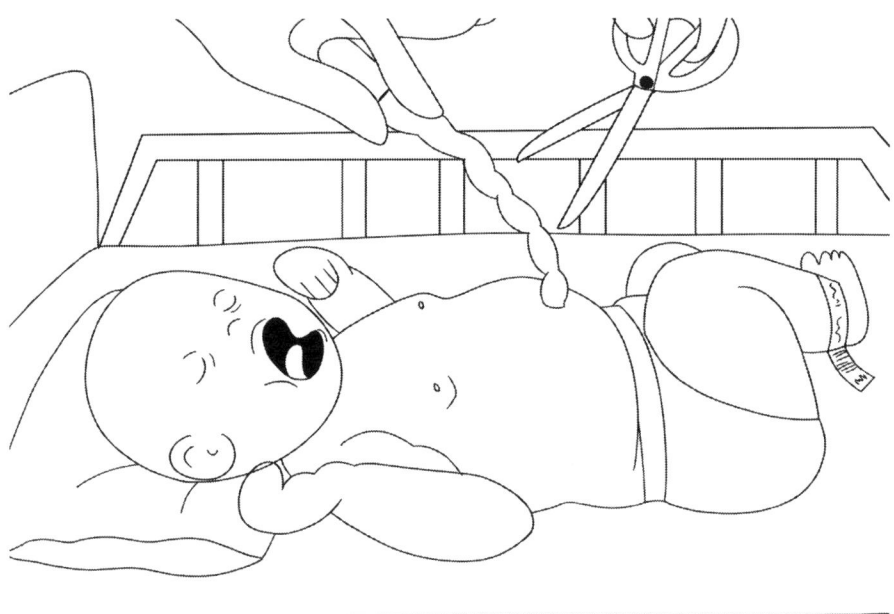

The phrase "cut the cord" means to end a connection with someone or something that had a protective/supportive role in one's life and to stop relying on it. The origin of this phrase stems from the act of human birth. When a baby is born, the umbilical cord that attaches the mother to the baby is cut. Once the cord is cut, the mother's body is no longer providing food through it to the baby. Instead, the baby is living and breathing on its own. Therefore, cutting the cord is a symbol of removing a protective and supportive bond.

73. Keen as mustard

To be "keen as mustard" means to be very excited and interested in something. We use this phrase to highlight someone's enthusiasm. It was first documented in William Walker's work called *Phraseologia Anglo-Latina, or phrases of the English and Latin tongue; together with Paroemiologia Anglo-Latina* in 1672. However, the connection can also be made with the meaning that the word "mustard" had in the early 20th century. The famous sauce was an essential element of roasted beef and became associated with intensity and enthusiasm because of its characteristic strong flavor. Therefore, when something was amazing, the common phrase was: "It's mustard!"

74. Dead as a doornail

To be "as dead as a doornail" is to be utterly dead or devoid of life. This expression can also be applied to an object that has become unusable. For example, a computer that cannot be started anymore because it is broken beyond repair can be called "as dead as a doornail." Furthermore, ideas or plans that are no longer possible can also be described as "dead as a doornail." This phrase was used in the 16th century by William Shakespeare and in Charles Dickens' *A Christmas Carol* in 1843. The expression probably originates from the method of securing doornails hammered into a door by clenching them.

75. Tall story

When we call someone's retelling of something a "tall story," it means that we consider it exaggerated and unnecessarily boastful. We usually use this idiom when we hear a story that's hardly possible or one that we don't believe at all. In that case, we can call it a "tall story," conveying to the person telling it that they should be more truthful in their storytelling.

76. Hit or miss

When something is "hit or miss," it means that it is sometimes successful/good and sometimes not, but we cannot rely on any outcome for certain, nor do we have any control over it. The expression most likely stems from some sort of shooting or throwing. It has been used in its present form since the 16th century, as it can be found in Shakespeare's *Troilus and Cressida*, which quotes: "But hit or miss, our project's life this shape of sense assumes."

77. Rain or shine

If a person is going to do something "rain or shine," it means that they are doing it whether it rains or not. However, the expression can also mean "no matter the obstacles" in some cases. In this instance, the phrase is used to state that the person is persistent about doing something, no matter what happens. The first recorded use of the expression was in 1699 by the writer John Goad.

78. Fight tooth and nail

To "fight tooth and nail" means to fight with all of one's effort and intensity. The phrase can be used to describe a physical fight or a verbal fight, but in both cases, it means that the opposing sides are giving it their all and that the conflict is very intense. This phrase comes from the idea of animals fighting as they use their teeth and nails to take down prey. The expression can be traced back to the 15th century, but connections can also be found between this idiom and the old Latin phrase "toto corpore atque omnibus ungulis" which translates to "all the body and with every nail."

79. Piece of cake

When something is a "piece of cake," it means that it is easy or requires little effort. A cake being related to something "easy" can be traced back to the 1870s. At that time, competitions called "cakewalks" were a common form of entertainment in the United States. In these contests, people tried to display who could walk the most gracefully. At the end of the competition, the most "graceful" pair would be given a cake as a reward. The tradition died out, and the term "cakewalk" eventually changed into the modern "piece of cake."

80. WHERE THE RUBBER MEETS THE ROAD

"Where the rubber meets the road" is a phrase that refers to a moment when a theory or idea is put to the test to see if it actually works. It can be translated to "a moment of truth" when things become clear and the observers can finally ascertain which ideas and assumptions were true and which weren't. It can also represent any moment when things become serious. The phrase is probably related to the imagery of the rubber wheels making contact with the road, representing the moment of truth when we can see if a vehicle is reliable or not.

Did you know?

There's a 107-acre forest made up of a single tree. The "Trembling Giant" in Utah's Fishlake National Forest includes over 47,000 quaking aspen trees that share the same root system. Some scientists estimate it's close to a million years old.

From the 16th century up until the 1960s, Egyptian mummies were actually ground up and used to produce a brown paint color called Mummy Brown. The powder was mixed with white pitch and myrrh to make a rich brown pigment.

The deepest mail box in the world is in a small Japanese fishing town called Susami, according to the Guinness Book of World Records. It's an old-school red mailbox that's located thirty-two feet (ten meters) under water, and divers often place waterproof letters there and they are then collected in regular intervals. The mailbox is quite active, as it receives one to five thousand pieces of mail annually.

It took almost twenty-two years to build the Taj Mahal in India. Construction began in 1632 and finished in 1653. It was built by Emperor Shah Jahan, who was in deep grief over his passing wife, as a tribute to their love.

81. Square peg in a round hole

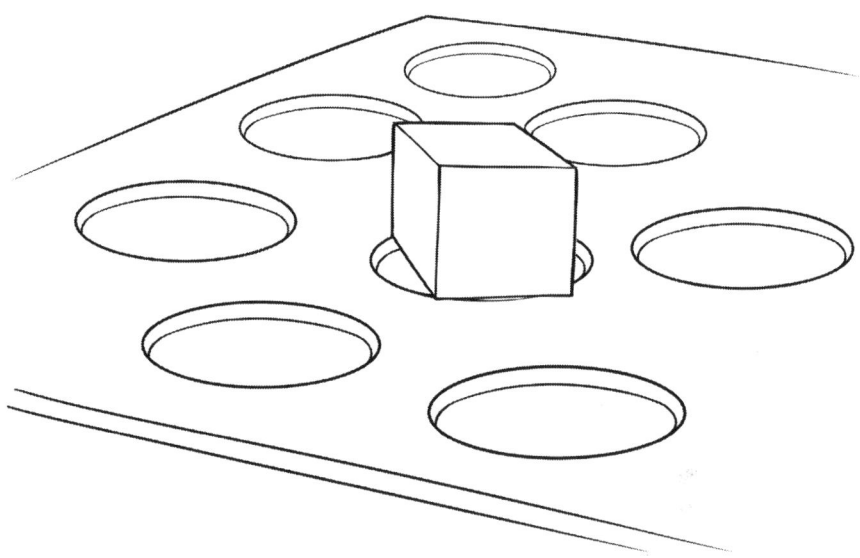

The phrase "square peg in a round hole" refers to a person in a situation unsuited to their abilities or character. Usually, we say that a person feels like a "square peg in a round hole" because they feel inadequate or like a misfit in a certain environment. This expression can be drawn back to the 19th century in England. A British philosopher and cleric by the name of Sydney Smith used it to describe someone who stood out or did not fit into society.

82. Pep talk

A "pep talk" refers to a talk that is meant to motivate or inspire. Usually, before doing something important, people give each other pep talks to encourage each other and better prepare for a coming challenge. Pep talks are common in sports, before games, but also in other competitive environments that require participants to stay motivated and focused. This term probably comes from the word "pepper" which was shortened to "pep" over time. In the 19th century, "pepper" was a symbol of personal energy or spirit. Since it was related to energy and motivation, in time it transformed into the modern phrase "pep talk."

83. Pie in the Sky

A "pie in the sky" refers to pleasant dreams of people that are not likely to come true. We use this idiom to describe a person's hopes that they fantasize about, but are far-fetched and hardly achievable. This phrase was first coined by the Swedish-American activist, Joe Hill, in 1911. He was using it as a way of criticizing the Salvation Army's philosophy, especially when it came to saving the souls of the hungry rather than providing them food. Rather than actually helping them, they were providing them with an illusion of happiness or a "pie in the sky."

84. Bob's your uncle

The term "Bob's your uncle" is another way of saying "it's as simple as that!" We use this phrase to conclude an explanation of a set of simple instructions or when a result is reached. By using this idiom, we convey that we consider the instructions straightforward and understandable. The origin of the phrase was connected to the events involving the British Prime Minister Robert Gascoyne-Cecil in 1887. That year, Prime Minister Robert, whose nickname was Bob, appointed his nephew, Arthur James Balfour, as the Minister of Ireland. For Arthur, it was simple to advance in position and status because "Bob was his uncle!" However, there is a big time lapse between these events and the popularization of this phrase, so the theory is far from confirmed.

85. All ears

The expression "I'm all ears!" means that someone is listening intently to what is being said and is dedicating their full attention to it. We use this phrase when we want to state that our attention is focused on what the person is saying. Sometimes, saying "we're all ears" is a way of putting the person who's about to speak in the spotlight and letting them know that everyone in the room is going to be quiet and listen to what they have to say. This phrase originated in the 18th century.

86. Night owl

A person who stays up very late at night or who does their best work at night is called a "night owl." We use this expression to describe a person whose active period happens during the night, who likes staying awake when it's dark outside. This phrase comes from the patterns and habits of actual owls as they sleep during the day and hunt for food at night.

87. Jack of all trades

A "jack of all trades" is a person who is skilled in many different areas and can do various types of work. We use this idiom as a compliment for a versatile person who can always contribute, no matter what the task is. However, there is a longer version of this idiom - "Jack of all trades, master of none." In this form, the expression is less of a compliment, because it conveys that the person is interested in many different areas of expertise, but because they are so diverse in their interests, they never committed themselves enough to master one of those skills. The phrase stems from the 14th century and is found in John Gower's poem *Confessio Amantis*.

88. Chew the fat

To "chew the fat" means to converse in a prolonged way and to take pleasure in it. It's usually a pleasant conversation between friends and acquaintances. For example, it's used when friends are gossiping together or telling stories from their pasts, and so on. There are multiple connections between this phrase and its origins. Chewing actual animal fat was done leisurely by the Northern American Native Americans. Farmers in Britain would also chew on pork fat when they were sitting and talking to others. It is even said that sailors did the same thing as a means of passing the time.

89. ON THE MEND

To mend something is to fix it, so if something is "on the mend," it means that it is either getting repaired or getting better. It usually refers to someone's health improving, but it can also be applied to other concepts, like when something that had deteriorated is in the process of getting back to its usual state, usually relationships between people. The idiom is based on the word "mend" which means "to repair" or "remove defects" and originates from the 13th century. This idiom has been applied with its meaning of improving health since the 1600s. It started to be used to describe an improvement in people's relationships in the 19th century.

90. Jump the Gun

To "jump the gun" means to act before one is supposed to or to do something too early without thinking it through first. We use this idiom to describe a person's hasty or reckless action or behavior. It is believed that this phrase is related to a gun being fired as a signal for the start of foot races or horse races. Competitors who started the race before the gun was fired were disqualified because they "jumped the gun" and went too early.

DID YOU KNOW?

Even though we associate Cleopatra with ancient Egypt, she actually lived during times that were closer to the invention of smartphones than the construction of the pyramids. Wooly mammoths were still walking around at the time when the Great Pyramid of Giza was finished.

The first ever decree about human rights was issued by Persian King Cyrus the Great in 539 B.C. The decree established the freeing of slaves, declared that all people had the right to choose their own religion, and established racial equality.

Cats walk like camels and giraffes: they move both of their right feet first, then move both of their left feet. No other animals walk this way.

Our brains have a primal gaze detection system that determines whether someone is staring directly at us or not. So next time you feel that someone is watching you, they probably are.

91. HALFWAY HOUSE

A "halfway house" is a term used to describe the midway point in a process. However, there is a second, more literal meaning of the phrase. Namely, "halfway house" is a center for the rehabilitation of people who lived in various institutions - former convicts, psychiatric patients, and other members of the society who are unaccustomed to life outside an institution. This phrase was first recorded in the 17th century. There is a story related to the phrase of a British public house that existed in the 1600s. This house was known as the *Old Red Lion Inn* and it was used by the young Princess Victoria as a halfway point between her voyages.

92. Bull's eye

When someone hits a "bull's eye," they hit the very center of a target. This phrase can be used as a literal term in target practice, or it can be used to describe a situation when a person answers a question or handles a situation perfectly. The term originated from 19th-century English shooting contests, probably because the black spot in the center of the target resembled the eye of a bull. The circles around the center represented how far the contestants were from the intended target or the center of the board. The shooter who hit the center was considered to have hit the "bull's eye."

93. On a Tear

The expression "on a tear" has multiple applications. Americans consider being "on a tear" as achieving great success continually, in which case they say that the person has been "on a tear" lately. The British meaning of doing something "on a tear" translates to doing something very quickly or having a sudden burst of energy. Its third, rarest use, is related to describing someone who is drinking heavily. The phrase stems from the 19th century and was used to refer to someone who was on a "drunken tear," meaning they drink a lot and "tear up the town." However, the phrase diverged from the drinking context into its present interpretation.

94. READ BETWEEN THE LINES

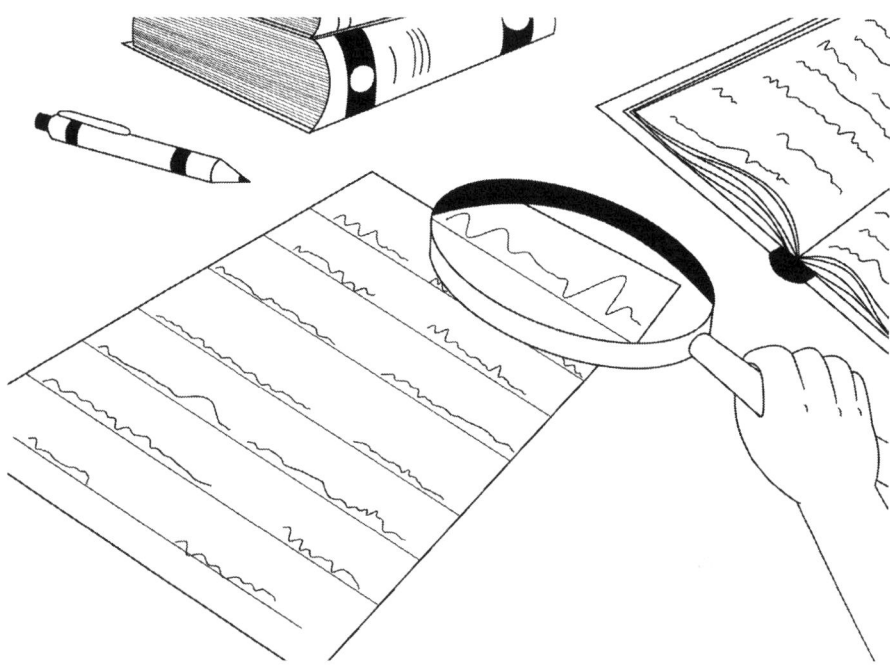

To "read between the lines" means to search for or find an implicit meaning of something written or said. We use this idiom to describe a situation when a message has more to tell us than the words on the surface. The implicit meaning that we are trying to point to is usually connected to people's real feelings or intentions that hide behind what they are saying. This expression derives from a simple form of cryptography in which a hidden meaning was conveyed by concealing it between lines of text.

95. Leg It

To "leg it" means to run very quickly, usually because the person running is being chased by someone else. We use this idiom to describe the action of running or fleeing, but also to invite someone to hurry up and start moving faster. The expression "use your legs" has been related to moving or speeding up one's movement since the 1500s. Over time, the phrase was shortened to just "leg it" as a quick way to tell someone to "move it."

96. Mum's the word

The expression "mum's the word" can be translated as "be quiet" or "say nothing." Even though the term "mum" is most commonly used as a shortened version of the word "mother," in this context it is referring to humming, or the noise one makes with their mouth closed. The sound of humming indicates an unwillingness or inability to speak. Therefore, when someone says "mum's the word," its meaning is "shut your mouth" as you would when you are "humming."

97. Means to an End

A "means to an end" is something done as a step towards achieving an ultimate goal. Often, the phrase is used to convey an action that is done with only the end goal in mind and doesn't consider the potential harm that might be caused along the way. In many cases, using this phrase implies dishonesty and having secret agendas, because the person is behaving in a certain way or using someone else for their personal goals. This phrase is drawn back to the field of Economics. In early Economics, the resources of the Earth were called "means" while human needs were called "ends."

98. Devil's Advocate

When someone is playing "devil's advocate," they are acting as if they are on the opposite side of the discussion or the debate to promote thought or create an argument. It can also refer to being mischievous, confusing, and introducing opposing thoughts just for the sake of it. This phrase was first brought into English in the 18th century as it was derived from the Latin phrase "advocatus diaboli." The first time it was used in its modern form was in a humorous text titled *Impostors Detected* in 1760.

99. Once Bitten Twice Shy

This proverb indicates that a negative experience causes people to be more cautious in the future. We use this proverbial saying in situations when people are being careful and guarded, so we assume that their past hurts or failures are the reason for it. A similar version of this proverb can be found in Eliza Fowler Haywood's novel *The History of Miss Betsy Thoughtless*, 1751, which quotes: "I have been bit once, and have made a vow never to settle upon any woman while I live, again."

100. TO THE NINES

"To the nines" can be translated as "to perfection" or "to the highest degree." We use this idiom to pay a compliment to how someone has completed something that they were aiming for and when we want to say "good job." In modern English, this compliment is most commonly paid regarding how the person is dressed; in such cases, we say that someone is "dressed to the nines" or "dressed up to the nines." The phrase is of Scottish origin. The earliest recorded sample of the expression is found in the 1719 *Epistle to Ramsay* by the Scottish poet William Hamilton.

101. WHEN IN ROME

The expression "when in Rome," which is followed by "do as Romans do," conveys that when a person is visiting a new place, they should follow the traditions of the culture that exists there. We often use this idiom in situations when a person is a tourist at a new and exotic destination with different customs, to encourage trying out new things. Furthermore, we can use it to state that a context or situation involves certain behavior and that it's for the best that we aspire to adapt to the context. The first printed use of this idiom can be traced back to 1777, in *Interesting Letters of Pope Clement XIV*.

Did you know?

In Greenland, the sun does not set from May 25th to July 25th. In the Arctic Circle, the midnight sun only lasts for about half an hour, but the further north you get, the longer it lasts. June 21, the longest day of the year, is a national holiday. July is the only month when Greenland's temperature reaches above freezing.

Chinese checkers wasn't actually invented in China, nor has a connection to any Asian country. The star-shaped marble game originated in Germany in 1892. When the game reached the United States, it started to be known as Chinese checkers, as American companies wanted to take advantage of the popularity of oriental imports.

The origin of the word "sinister" reflects a historical bias against left-handed people. It comes from the Latin word for "left," which was also seen to be unlucky or evil.

In the 1700s, coins were actually made of real gold and silver. Often criminals would shave down the sides of the coins and sell the shavings. Consequently, the US Mint began adding ridges to the coins, a process called reeding, to make it impossible to shave down without being detected, while also making counterfeiting more difficult. Today, no coins are made from precious metals, but the tradition has continued on coins of higher value. The reeding also helps the visually impaired to tell the difference between coins.

Bonus

Thanks for supporting me and purchasing this book! I'd like to send you some freebies. They include:

- The digital version of *500 World War I & II Facts*
- The digital version of *101 Idioms and Phrases*
- The audiobook for my best seller *1144 Random Facts*

Scan the QR code below, enter your email and I'll send you all the files. Happy reading!

Check out my other books!